THE CHURCH WHO PRODUCED MILLIONAIRES

How You Can Be Successful and Still Love God

Dr. Sandra N. King

Website: www.drsandranking.com

ISBN: 979-8-9919269-0-4

Publishing Support Services by:

Motivational M.D. Enterprises
www.imreadytolaunch.com

TABLE OF CONTENTS

DEDICATION v

ACKNOWLEDGMENTS vi

INTRODUCTION 7

CHAPTER 1 -- BE THE LIGHT OF THE WORLD AND SALT OF THE EARTH 9

CHAPTER 2 -- ACTIVATE YOUR FAITH 21

CHAPTER 3 -- UNDERSTAND THE POWER OF PRAYER 29

CHAPTER 4 -- BE HUMBLE 39

CHAPTER 5 -- GIVE YOUR TITHES 44

CHAPTER 6 -- STAY CONNECTED TO THE SOURCE 50

CHAPTER 7 -- FIND THE CHURCH WHO PRODUCES MILLIONAIRES 60

CLOSING REFLECTIONS 66

DISCUSSION QUESTIONS 67

ABOUT THE AUTHOR 70

NOTES 71

DEDICATION

I am dedicating this book to my daddy and mommy. Both of you always believed that I could do anything under 2 conditions: First, I have to be the best at whatever it is that I want to do. You told me if I wanted to be the best street sweeper, (even though we no longer have actual street sweepers due to modern technology), that I am to be the best, whatever it is that I am to leave a mark so great that not only that it cannot be erased, but it can never be duplicated. Second, whatever I put my mind to, do it. I would like to dedicate this to my children. My three parts of my heart, my mind (Dee), my heart (Touuu) and my mouthpiece (Butta). I love you all and you complete me. To my brothers, Sam, Vic and Joe, thanks.

It is because of you all that I am here and living my dreams.
Thank you.

ACKNOWLEDGMENTS

I would like to acknowledge my teacher from the 8th grade, Mrs. Methvin. She was the first person who gave me my first writing assignment. She was surprised that it was written well by me and from there I was motivated to write. I would like to acknowledge the Puryear family. You all have been and are a staple for me since my dad's transition. You all opened your homes and your hearts to me and my children.

I would like to acknowledge the Dent family. You all showed me how to persevere when things aren't going as I planned even though there were things in place for me to prosper.

I would like to also acknowledge my Pastors because God has truly led me to them. From them, I learned about the Bible and how to apply it to my life to get God-given results.

I would also like to acknowledge Mrs. Anderson who made sure that I knew how to be a young lady and how to hand over scissors correctly.

I would like to acknowledge Vonzella Abrams as the first leader in my life besides my mom and teachers. From you Vonzella, I learned how to be a strong leader and use my mind to achieve whatever I want to achieve.

I would like to acknowledge Dr. Jaz for helping me to birth this book. Because of you, I can now rest because this book is completed. Now I am waiting for the vision to become complete.

To everyone on this page, you all have made such a powerful impact in my life that has lasted me for over 25 years.

Thank you.

INTRODUCTION

My name is Sandra, and the reason why I decided to write this story is because of a little girl who believed everything that people told her. She believed what people said about her not being able to preach, that she would be nothing more than just nothing. She believed the circumstances of what she saw. What she was seeing at the time were the circumstances of being a single mom on welfare, with too many baby daddies, etc. She wanted to be a doctor. She wanted to be a writer. She wanted to be an entrepreneur and comedian. She wanted to be so much more. Well, eventually she, meaning me, became all these things. When I got a bit older, there was something so significant that I learned and I just have to share it.

Here is what I have been taught: The power to define is the power to fulfill. What do I mean by that? How does someone know when they are looking at a rose? I mean, I was taught that a rose is red, it has a lovely fragrance, and that women love roses. I was taught all the beautiful things of a rose, but what I wasn't taught that roses hurt! Meaning, they have those little prickly things on them that when handled incorrectly, would cause pain and bleeding! I wasn't taught that. I also wasn't taught that roses come in many colors! But how was I supposed to know that there are white roses, pink roses, and yellow roses unless someone sat me down and gave me the whole truth as to what a rose is and the different varieties of it? How was I supposed to know that those prickly things on a rose, which I now know are thorns, had many purposes? Purposes such as a defense against the animals who eat them. Or, that a great purpose of the thorns which are on the rose are what the roses need. Another need for thorns is that the rose uses the thorns to climb so the rose can get proper sunlight because roses grow in bushes. I had to learn all these details on my own. I had to learn that roses hurt and that they come in many colors. What I did was, I added to what I was initially told and taught about a rose, which is that roses are red and that they have a lovely fragrance. I also added my own experience. Once I had an encounter with the rose, I realized that they don't hurt because I learned how to handle the rose. I was no longer in pain and I no longer bled because I learned the uses of the thorns. I love the white roses mixed with pink roses and they don't even have a fragrance that I was once taught that they have. Side Note: If anyone wants to send me white roses, I will accept them. *Just kidding :)*

I learned that the power to define is the power to fulfill. I want to further add that once the power to define has been fulfilled, then now I have the ability and permission to walk in both my predestined truth and unquestionable power. Let's take for example the word 'millionaire'. After all, the title of the book is "The Church Who Produced Millionaires". There is one word that will be focused on and that word is 'millionaire'. From my research, the word 'millionaire' is a noun, which means it describes a person, place, or thing. Not to insult intelligence, I am going somewhere with this. Breaking down the word 'millionaire', it is a known fact that it involves money or some sort of numerical value. The word suffix 'Aire' means someone who has a legal right to an inheritance, either by adoption or by blood, meaning families such as the Vanderbilts or Rockefellers. This book will do just that. It will get you in the mindset that the 'church' can, will, and has the tools to produce 'millionaires. Now, let's get into it! Are you ready??? Let's

goooooooooooooooooooooooooooooooooooooooooooooooo
oooooooo!!!!!

CHAPTER 1

BE THE LIGHT OF THE WORLD AND SALT OF THE EARTH

How appropriate for this being the first chapter of this book. Be the salt of the earth. First, let us examine salt. Have you noticed that salt has been given a warning label reputation lately? What a warning label reputation is, that once something has been 'discovered' to cause an adverse effect, or that something is linked to an adverse effect, then the label is out. In other words, a bad reputation. I was putting it nicely. An example of a warning label reputation is that salt causes edema, or swelling of the is. Another one is that salt causes weight gains due to water retention.

Salt has some good uses, such as being used as a preservative to prolong shelf time. It has also been used to clean wounds and break up ice. For those of us who decided to live where there is snow and ice every single year, we tend to sprinkle

Morton's table salt on the steps or walkways to our homes. This technique breaks up the ice and causes the snow to melt. Now, for the rest of the population that lives where it doesn't snow or have ice, I am moving there. Just joking! Going back a little bit, remember the definition of millionaire, that it is a noun, right? Having salt is not a bad thing. Being asked to be the salt of the earth or the light of the world can be both confusing and misleading if taken literally. Now, with salt, in my opinion, it makes food taste better. If cooked correctly, salt can be well appreciated. If too much salt is applied, then the food will not taste good. It will be almost like an old, stiff flavor, and not the soft or palatable flavor that one seeks when cooking food. But what about the salt-free salt? Before I move forward, you are probably asking yourself, how do I know that having or cooking in too much salt will make the food stiff or stale tasting? Well, actually I found this out from personal experience. It was the beginning of my cooking career. I was newly married, for the first time, and I had 2 children. Imagine me calling my mom for her meatloaf recipe. She gives me the ingredients to make her meatloaf. Her ingredients were 1 pound of ground meat, bread crumbs, 1 egg, tomato paste, and salt. I asked her how much salt, and she said enough salt to taste. Now, I am not going to taste raw meat, it's just nasty to me. Some people think it is a delicacy. However, I asked her how do I know if I was putting little salt in the food, or, if I was putting too much in the food? Can you guess what she told me? She told me to do what she had instructed me to do until I got the taste that I desired, and this is after I have cooked the meatloaf. And that is what 'being the salt of the earth' means.

My mother gave me a strong piece of advice that will forever be cemented in my brain and that is…if the food is too salty...throw it away because it is good for nothing but for high blood pressure, headache, and you being labeled as a horrible cook. That means, if anyone knows that you have cooked a dish, it will not be touched. Once again, I am speaking from experience. If I could give you a word of advice, it is that you have to follow instructions!

Following instructions seemed to be a forgotten art. It appears that everyone wants to be a leader and not a follower. Being a follower means a lot to leaders. Just look at the social media platforms…followers = success. And the same is true in this case. It all depends on who you follow.

Followers are essential because they are the watchers of the wall. Meaning, they are able to see what is or isn't going on. Followers can see what the leaders don't see or aren't able to see because the leaders are busy leading. If you were to have a social media platform, you would see where the leader of a page or group employs administrators. These administrators are the keepers who are on the wall. Do you know where they get these administrators from? From their followers. What do followers do? They follow instructions. Some rules must be followed which are there for a reason. There are certain people who would like to know why the rules were created. Sometimes and in certain circumstances, the followers don't need to know why the rules were made. On the other hand, the reason as to why must be revealed.

Let us look at some fun facts about salt:

1. Salt was the currency back in ancient times because it was the most expensive and most abundant, especially in Rome.
2. It is an ESSENTIAL element of your body. Here's a quick anatomy lesson. Salt is needed as one of the elements that helps regulate the nerves in your body. It also helps with the muscles of your body, especially the heart.
3. If used correctly, salt is a great purifier other than fire.

There are many, many uses for salt and how precious it is which is why I think that the explanation of becoming the salt of the earth is a great example of how to be of an influence in this world. Let's look at these 3 main reasons about how you can become the salt of the earth.

1. As stated previously, salt was the most expensive form of currency in ancient times. If I were to correct one word in the previous sentence, it would be the word 'was'. The word 'was' means past tense and humans are not past tense. You are and never will be a past tense. Even after the body ceases to function, there will always be the memory of you. This means, in essence, YOU ARE EXPENSIVE!!! Even artificial intelligence (AI) still requires human intervention. Meaning, YOU ARE ESSENTIAL!!! Look at it like this; anyone can rebuild a car and it will cost around $30,000 to build it brand new, depending on the make and model of the car. This can be the same with a house being built but it would be more expensive, probably around $250,000 and above, with the blueprints that are needed to build it. But not the human body, NOT YOU! The only way to build a

human being is through and by a human being, and not by blueprint.

You see, it is easy to replace or rebuild parts of a car or a house. With regards to a human being, the parts can only come from a human being. You know what else? As a species, meaning humans, we are in abundance. Now, whether or not we all get along, is another book for another day, but be the salt. Be the one that when a person encounters a bite into a delicious entree of food, and that person says, "This is savory and delicious, I want another bite", you can be the same way. When people encounter you, they should be saying, "Wow, their energy motivates me to be better", or, "When I first spoke to you, I was in a bad mood. After speaking with you, I do not feel mad or sad. Thank you." This is what being the salt and light of the earth means. Whoever you encounter, just know that YOU are the salt that is needed. YOU are the expensiveness that is irreplaceable. As a matter of fact, if you are reading up to this point, you can become even more irreplaceable by making sure that YOU become an everlasting, positive, or outstanding memory. That encounter should be so life changing, that will become ingrained in their minds...forever.

2. Salt is ESSENTIAL for the body to function, especially for the operation of the nerves. YOU are ESSENTIAL because the world NEEDS YOU! Yep, I said it. I NEED YOU...you have the spice that is needed to turn things upside down. Why, you may ask? Because no one on

this planet has the same qualities as YOU and no one on this planet has the same talents as YOU. Yes, YOU! For example, let's take a person who has the occupation of a barber. There may be 50,000 barbers in the state where you live. They may have invented a cut that will forever revolutionize the barber industry. That's the salt. As there are many types of salt like kosher salt, sea salt, Hawaiian salt and table salt, there are many different types of people with many different talents that are needed to make the world a better place.

3. How does salt purify? Salt can purify the air by getting rid of or neutralizing the pollutants in the air, thus, reducing allergy symptoms and helping those who have asthma to breathe easier. I'm not saying to throw salt up in the air and it purifies, no, what I am saying is that sodium is in the air in minute, or tiny amounts. This 'salt air' as it is commonly referred to, comes off of the sea. I live almost 150 miles from the Atlantic Ocean. It is amazing how the wind will blow the smallest of salt to purify the air, so it is with YOU. It doesn't matter how small you may think your talent is, that talent is needed to make the change that we need for the world. For you to build YOUR dreams. To complete your God given assignment.

The light of the world. As stated previously, light extinguishes darkness. Light can also give direction. For example, when there is a ship at sea, they look for a beacon of light that rotates. Looking for this light gives the ship captain not only direction but hope. Is it difficult being the light in a dark situation? Yes! But you can become the light in a difficult situation by doing the proverbial cliche. The proverbial cliche is this: do unto others as YOU would want them to do unto YOU. I would like to add: do good in all that you do, even when no one is looking. But how though?

As I am writing this book, I also reflect upon my actions. There was a time when I was totally opposite of being the 'salt of the earth, the light of the world'. I was a horrible person who didn't care what you said about me because I knew how to make you look like a bad person. I would act in such a manner that those who didn't know me would be like, 'She couldn't act like that' and to those who did know me, would be like, 'Yep, that is her. She acts totally like that'. I mean, it was so bad that both my daddy and brothers would warn those who I dated by saying, "Are you sure you want to date her? You know she is crazy, right?" So, how was I horrible? Now, this is me and how I was horrible. My example may not be suited for you; this is just an example of how I was. I would start fights, and in some cases I would finish them. I didn't care who you were, old or young. I wouldn't tip my waitresses even though I was a waitress. I would steal cars, lie, and cheat (on tests in high school and on my husbands). By the time I was 21, I was so sexually promiscuous I had over 25 lovers, which means that I lost my virginity at a very early age, winginly. Yes, I was a garden utensil. The only thing that I didn't do was drink and smoke. Go figure huh?

So, how did I become expensive, in abundance, able to make food taste better, and a useful person? I did it in the following steps. Now, these steps can be difficult, they can be a challenge, or they can be easy. It all depends on you. First, it is the mind, then the heart, and lastly, accountability. Let's look at all 3 of these.

1. I made up my mind that I was going to do it. The strongest muscle in the human body is the mind. The human brain houses thought, balance (meaning movement), creativity, and homeostasis (balance between inside the body and the outside environment). When someone passes on, or when a person is pronounced dead, the human brain remains active for 7 minutes after the heart has finished beating. Now that is powerful!

   I realized how nasty I was to my fellow man. I realized that using the driving 'finger' may get me injured or killed. I realized that the mess that was inside of me was maneuvering its way to the outside. This mess was making its way to my house and was causing my home to become a mess. It was such a mess that my children were threatening to be taken away from me. So, I had to become my own salt. I changed how I talked to people. No matter how people treated me, or how they talked to me, I had to become the 'bigger' person. I had to be willing to change how I was thinking because I was going nowhere fast. In doing so, I became the salt that was needed.

   I remember when someone I was close to told me that they wished they had the positivity that I present at work. I told them that I made up my mind to be positive. It took time and a lot of work, but I did it.

2. Once I made up my mind that I was going to become the salt that I needed in my life, I then purposed it in my heart. This means that whatever I decide to do to change my life to become salt, my body will line up with it. For example, my mother and I rarely saw eye to eye growing up. I remembered that my father told me to respect my mother. Believe me, it was a challenge. However, following my father's death, that is what I did. Purposing it in my heart gave me my why. It gave me a reason to be respectful. When I have a disagreement with someone and in this case my mother, my voice no longer gets loud nor does my tone or language get disrespectful. I had to remember to honor my parents because I want to go to heaven so I can have a nice life. I want to see how perfect heaven is. Because I had purposed it in my heart, my voice did not get loud. My mouth wouldn't even form the words that I wanted to say sometimes because I wanted to say them.

   Another example is when I was cut off in traffic one day which resulted in me almost running into a barrier. I was scared. Before I purposed in my heart, I would curse them out as I was driving erratically to catch them while using the 'driving finger'. This is where I was talking about almost getting killed. I needed to stop behaving in such a manner, especially when my kids were in the car. That person in the car who did that to me, I had to let them go. I had to realize that I cannot control the thoughts or the actions of other people, I can only control my thoughts and actions. When one purposes in their heart to change, these are the decisions that will become easier to make.

3. Having accountability. This can be the most difficult to accomplish. I have realized that in my life, accountability in everyday life is weaning. What do I mean by 'weaning'? I simply mean that accountability is hard to come by. Who wants to be reminded of what they intend to do? Who wants to be told what to do when you are grown and have been doing life on your own? No one. However, being accountable to someone, a person who knows you well, or someone that you may have paid like a counselor or therapist, can be extremely beneficial. Being held accountable makes life easy.

There are people who can help people who are called accountability partners. Accountability partners are people that you choose to hold you accountable to the area that you want to change. Those who have decided to kick the drug habit are a great example of an accountability partner. They are called sponsors. If they know what their triggers are and if they decide to take a drink or smoke or whatever vice they may have, the accountability partner stops them from indulging by reminding them of why they are becoming sober. I needed my accountability partner to remind me of what my father told me how I should treat my mother. I also needed to be reminded that I could not drive that way because my kids would be the injured party.

Can I ask you a question? In what areas of your life can you become the salt of the earth? In what area of your life can you change to become the salt of the earth? Being the salt of the earth doesn't mean to change in grandiose style. It can be something as small as letting someone over in traffic. It can be when someone cuts in line in front of you at the grocery store, and you let them take it. I understand that there are times when you can't be nice, that is in another book. You can still be the salt of the earth while not being a pushover. That is also not what I am asking of you. I am asking for every one of us to become the salt of the earth. You are the answer to what the world needs, and that is love.

MOMENT OF REFLECTION:

A moment of reflection is nothing more than a time to yourself. Take this time to just breathe, look around at your surroundings and be grateful for what you do have in your life. There are many people who don't have what you have, maybe your next-door neighbor, you don't know. Reflect on the areas of your life that can be lifted up and the ones that you are proud of. Reflect on the areas that you can improve in. Remember, it doesn't have to be something huge, only if you want it to be. It can be small, like letting someone over in traffic without giving the traffic finger. Believe it or not, small things truly do add up.

CHAPTER 2

ACTIVATE YOUR FAITH

The previous chapter talked about being the salt of the earth, a savory person. Well, let us continue, shall we? Looking at the word activate, it is a common understanding that the meaning of the word activate means to make something or cause something that wasn't active to become active, or to cause something to move. Let us use a credit card as an example. To use my credit card, I must first activate it, or, take it from a state of not being active to becoming active or to move it from a state of not being able to move. There are a couple of things that I must do in order for me to even get a credit card.

1. I have to look to see the type of credit card that I want. There are many credit card companies with varying interest rates. There are credit cards that are secured and unsecured. There are credit cards that have an annual fee and those that don't. My favorites are the

ones that have the flier miles (I still have yet to get one of those but when I do...)

2. I must apply. In order for me to apply, I must first see if I meet the qualifications. There were so many times that I applied for a credit card and I got denied because of my credit score. It was so bad I couldn't get the Xfinity free cable. Old Navy has a credit card for those who are just starting out. It was mainly for credit builders. Let's just say that I didn't get that one either. But I had to do the work and fill out the application.

3. Then there's Visa, MasterCard, American Express, Diner's Club, Star, and a few others. I have to decide and research which credit card is accepted everywhere, not just in some places. There are some places that may not accept Diners Club or American Express.

In using the example of credit cards, there are 3 key points that need to be discussed in order for activation to be made.

A. Decide.
B. Apply.
C. Now, GO, do it.

A. **Decide**.

Making a decision is very important because once the mind is made up, the body and the universe will comply. What do I mean by that? I believe that the mind is the strongest muscle in the human body. The mind, or the brain, controls thinking, moving, and breathing just to name a few. Another importance is that it is responsible for all the successes that you or I may ever want and have. It is the mind where creativity lies, where the seat of imagination occurs.

There is a saying that says if you can think it, it can be achieved. I believe in this saying. There is also another saying that says as a man thinks within his heart, he can be it. In this instance, the heart is the mind. Ironically enough, both the heart and the mind work in concert with each other. Whatever you think, whatever you believe, and whatever you focus on, will become a reality for expansion.

Once a mind is made up, there is no turning back. There is no wishy-washiness. Once the mind is made up, there is a certain concreteness that happens. There is a certain confidence that has been awakened. It does not matter what obstacle in life may throw at an individual, that individual will find a way to not only navigate through that obstacle but also keep on track to accomplish whatever they have made up their mind to do. For example, when I decided to enter the United States Army, I was older than a lot of other recruits and have experienced life more than others. I was married and had a family. Was I told that I was too old to go into the Army? Was I told that they don't prefer older women? Yes. Guess who the people were who told me that I was too old to join the Army. Guess who it was that told me I did not belong in the Army because I was a married woman and mother. It was those who had no affiliation whatsoever with the Army. Some of them were strongly opposed to me entering the Army because of who was in office at the time.

I had a decision to make. I decided to either listen to what those people were saying or, look at my family dynamics. I chose to look at my own family dynamics because I had to be able to provide for them and break any generational curses that were, and still are, on my first family, meaning my mom, dad, and brothers. That is another topic for another book. What I have learned from making this decision is that once my mind is made up, it is a done deal. Another thing I learned is that it doesn't matter who has opinions, it is me who decides. Decisions make actions that are a direct reflection of faith because it is faith that one looks at in hopes of accomplishing the decision that has been made.

B. Apply.

Going back to what was said earlier, in the example of the credit cards. I chose which credit card I wanted, and I chose Visa. Once I chose, I then applied with the company of my choice. I had to apply action. In this case, I will say that it is the definition of applying, but as a noun definition, it will be considered application. Application means to put into practice what you have been taught or to put into practice what you know. This is most difficult to achieve because oftentimes people are given what to do but are not given how to do it. This often causes a stagnation of the application. Not knowing how to apply the knowledge of what you received, can be extremely frustrating. It can be frustrating to the point that the information you have attained may appear to be bogus. Sometimes it is, but it is still information that can be used.

When applying, an individual can do this by also applying faith. Well, what is faith? The Bible describes faith in Hebrews 11:1 as being the substance of things hoped for, the evidence of things not seen. Here, faith is the substance. How can faith be a substance? Well, what is substance? Substance is described as the real physical matter of which a person or thing consists and which has a tangible, solid presence. It is the stuff that makes substance. A substance is something that can be held, touched, observed, and used. Faith is the activation that brings the substance to the individual who wants it. Notice that there are 2 words here: faith and hope. Hope is a feeling of expectation and desire for a certain thing to happen. Putting it together, when an individual has a desire to change their life with a certain expectation that they want to see, then the faith comes in by doing what they know to do to have an expected outcome. This is how the application is accomplished.

Faith will cause you to seek out the necessary change. Sometimes, seeking out how to change may cause a person to go to seminars, read books, attend church services, or go to therapy. Once the way or the avenue is now clear for the person who is seeking change, then the application can begin. This will cause the evidence, the seeking, the application, the hope, and the substances, to now be seen. When looking at someone successful, they are only looking at the finished product. When I look at Steve Harvey or Jeff Bazos, I am only looking at the finished product of their avenues to success. I didn't see when Steve Harvey was homeless and only had 200 dollars to do an amateur night at the Apollo. I didn't see Jeff Bezos in his garage selling products only to see him CEO of Amazon quintessentially becoming one of the wealthiest human beings on the planet.

I only came up with these two individuals on the fly. I know that there are plenty of others I could have used, however, they used applications so that their hopes and dreams could have the expected outcome that they desired. Oftentimes, when people look at those who are extremely successful, they are looking at the success, which is the tip of the iceberg. They are only looking at the good end of their success, not the messy journey. They didn't see the sleepless nights. They didn't see the naysayers that kept them from having their dreams come true. It is through these times that their application became of the utmost importance.

C. Once a decision has been made, and once the application has been established, just do whatever it takes.

Now, I must say that it is up to the individual who wants to have a positive change in their life. By this step, the individual has overcome any naysayers, they have evaluated their current situation and just decided to do it. Any application that is needed, has already been researched and established. Just do it.

There was a time in my life when I had to apply everything in this chapter. Back in 2012, I ended up being a homeless veteran. I had my children with me. I trusted someone who I wasn't supposed to trust. At this time, I had to first decide what I was going to do. Was I going to just let me and my children stay where we are, meaning being in a homeless shelter, or, get up and find the resources to be able to change our current situation? I decided that I was going to change my family's situation, which was the first step.

Next, I had to apply the resources that I knew of. I knew how to get on food stamps, so I did. From there, I used the resources that they had, meaning my social worker, to get my family into a place. So, I applied to get into my apartment. Then, I enrolled in college to get my nursing degree. I didn't finish my nursing degree, but I did go to cosmetology school, and I opened up a hair salon. Application can also come from the things that have happened in your life, however, take from situations where you can learn from because life is a school and the experiences are textbooks. Because I decided, applied, and just did it, I realized a deeper strength within me, and that is I can do anything, absolutely ANYTHING, that comes to my mind. This is activating my faith.

Being empowered with deciding, applying, and doing is POWERFUL. Remember that these 3 steps can be done with something as small as allowing someone over in traffic to something as big as starting a billion-dollar company. If there is a call to action, it would be to just decide and everything will line up.

MOMENT OF REFLECTION:

Remember a time when there was a decision in your life that needed to be made. What type of decision was it? Was it something that you needed to write a book, sing a song, call a loved one, or get a house, it doesn't matter. When it is something that is over like 25 years ago, don't give up on it. Decide, apply, and do it. Remember, as long as you are doing these things, you are activating faith.

CHAPTER 3

UNDERSTAND THE POWER OF PRAYER

What is prayer? Prayer is communication. It is communication between an individual and their deity. In my case, it will be communication between me and God. In America, there are approximately 10,989,000 million people who don't pray. I have realized that when America either comes under attack or when there is a natural disaster or anything horrible that has happened, the first response is prayer. There are times, regardless of who the President is or what fundamental religious beliefs the President may have, the President will ask the Americans to pray.

Prayer is powerful. It does not have to be long and drawn out, it can be something as simple as, "Jesus, protect me and my family", just six words. If a person wants to pray, they can make it as long as they want to. The main idea of prayer is communication.

Remember, communication is a two-way dialogue that has components. It is like this: the sender sends a message and the receiver responds to the message. Within this sending and receiving, there is a technique that I try to enhance, which at times can be very difficult and that is listening. In order for the receiver to send a message back, the receiver must first listen to what the sender is sending to get a proper response.

There is a phenomenon that says people listen to respond instead of listening to understand. What listening to respond instead of listening to understand means, is that people listen to what is being said. They only pick what they want to respond to. It is like they don't care about the feelings behind what is being said because they only care about themselves. For communication to be effective, the verbal and nonverbal must both be heard.

There is no real rhyme or reason as to how to pray. What is important is that prayer happens. To me, there is a way that I pray and the acronym that I use is P.R.A.Y.E.R. which means purpose, relationship, acknowledgment/availability, yielding, easy and results. For purpose, what is the nature of the prayer? Why is prayer needed at that time? Sometimes, it could be just to say hi to the higher deity, or, there is a serious situation where prayer is needed.

Purpose decides the nature of the prayer. Is it going to be an earnest prayer (importance, imminent need), a hello prayer (like, hey God, how are you doing today? Do you see what is going on here today?) or, is it a thank you prayer (thank you God for allowing me to see another day of not cursing out anyone or using my driving finger). Now, by no means are these the types of prayers. This section is not a formal section of prayer. That will be in another book. The purpose of this section is to bring awareness of prayer and that prayer isn't difficult to achieve at all.

Relationship. When communicating, there is an established relationship. It can be a relationship of which it is husband and wife, mother and child, employer and employee. There is communication that is within relationships. In order for a relationship to survive, there must be communication. Without communication, there is no relationship, which means the relationship dies.

This is true of prayer. Having a relationship is so much more important than having a 'religionship'. Here is what I mean. For example, when my children were smaller, they would cry. To me, all cries of children are the same but I know my child's cry, or when they say, "Momma", that I will answer immediately. I will not answer to another child when they are calling for their momma. That is because I have a relationship with children, I do not have a relationship with that child. For instance, if my child was on the field at basic training where everyone looked the same, dressed the same, and stood the same, I did not have to walk the field to look for my child. When they marched upon the field, I would spot my child because I knew how they walked, how they stood, and how they looked regardless of how indoctrinated the military may have groomed them to be.

In a 'religionship', religion says that I must pray in this manner, every time I pray. 'Religionship' says that doctrination is the law and not having a relationship with God. 'Religionship' also states that prayer can only be done at church. And I have to add, that what we call the church isn't the church. This will be discussed later.

'Religionship' says that tradition is the standard, where a relationship goes against tradition. 'Religionship' says that the Pastor is the Pastor and that, in some cases, there isn't any accountability. However, relationship says that is not so! Accountability is paramount.

When a relationship is established, then communication is clear, concise and accurate. When the people who are in dialogue with each other know each other's voice, along with knowing their nonverbal cues, it makes it easier to communicate. Oftentimes, people ask, "How do I know when God is talking to me?" A better question to ask is, "Have I spoken to God today?" Once someone is in a relationship, the voice will become unmistakable, and knowing how someone behaves is a key point.

Relationship says that temperament is known and behavior is understood. Temperament is how someone thinks, how they are originally after they leave work, when they get home and unwind, and their idiosyncrasies. Once that is established, then the behavior should mirror what is being displayed.

Acknowledgment availability. In order for prayer to occur, is there any availability? Being available is the intimacy of the relationship. This is the same for prayer. Having availability means that time is carved out and there is a consideration of thoughts, feelings, and words that are followed by actions.

Acknowledgment means that the presence of God is there. It means that your purpose is a part of your acknowledgment.

Acknowledging the other party shows respect. It shows concern. It shows honor. These are also key aspects of relationships and communication.

Acknowledgment also means that you are acknowledging the other person's feelings, thoughts, and concerns. Acknowledgment is mainly for the sending party. Acknowledgment mainly is the first thing that is not said by the sender. In this case, the sender would send out a concern or a thought, which I would call a tester, to gauge the way that the conversation would go. Acknowledgment is more like the barometer, or temperature gauge, that will direct or guide the conversation.

So how does acknowledgment become a part of prayer? According to the King James Bible, God created all human beings. Which means, we are all made in the image of Him. We have His feelings because He created us. He is the Creator so the creation should acknowledge Him. Look at it another way. Everyone has a set of parents. It should be customary to acknowledge them from time to time. Or, in a significant other relationship, if it is husband-wife, girlfriend-boyfriend, or common law, acknowledgment is needed. In either of the above-mentioned relationships, if there is no acknowledgment, then the relationship's communication channel will be greatly stiffened.

How can an acknowledgment be achieved in prayer? Simply by acknowledging God. This can be done by saying something along the lines of, "Father God, I know you exist. I know that you are everywhere". But what if you don't know this information about God, if you even think that God exists, you can still say the same thing.

Yielding. As a driver, we are taught to yield when we see a yellow light, at the yield sign, or when giving the right of way. This is the same in prayer. When a person yields in prayer, they are allowing themselves to yield from the day's activities, yielding to life and yielding to God. What do I mean by yielding to God? It means giving your full, undivided attention to your time with God. There should be nothing that will be a distraction. There are times when I pray when or as I drive. I don't close my eyes, as tradition may have it. When in communication, both parties should give their undivided attention to each other. As the sender, they are yielding what they are saying in how they are saying it. They should yield towards how the receiving party will receive the message they are saying. As the receiver, they should yield in how they respond to the sender's message. It is here in the yielding where both parties' attitudes should be checked and listening to comprehend instead of listening to respond should be paramount.

Easy. Keep it simple. All people should be doing when praying is to talk in your normal way of talking. If, for example, a person speaks Spanish, then Spanish is what God understands. If an individual speaks broken English, then God understands. If the individual speaks Creole, then God will understand. Whatever language an individual speaks, God will understand it. What is easy is that the individual talks, God listens, then God talks and the individual listens.

Results. Once purpose has been established or known; once a relationship has been established; acknowledgment/availability is on board; and yielding has been occurring. If you make the language of your prayer easy then results are destined to happen. It has been taught that God will give you the desires, or requests, of your heart. Now, whoever preaches this must understand that yes, God does give the desires or requests of our heart. However, it must also be taught that the answered request may not come in the way that we are looking for it to be given. The thing about results is that the individual must be patient.

These components are what make prayer powerful. There was a time in my life when I prayed to become a doctor. I was in high school at that time. I went to my guidance counselor and told her that I wanted to become a doctor. She told me that because I had a grade point average of 2.65, I would not even be considered for medical school. That set me back like 20 years. Then along the way, I realized that there are several doctors that I could become. PhDs, MDs, DDS, etc. I decided to research which doctor I wanted to become and that was a PhD. I chose the school and did the work. I had my relationship established and I acknowledged God and made myself available to hear from Him and made sure that I had time in my schedule to complete the coursework, including a dissertation. I yielded myself to be able to hear and to quiet what my guidance counselor spoke to me 20+ years ago. I made my prayer easy by talking to God the way I would speak to my family and close friends. My result: today I am Dr. Sandra N. King.

If I could empower someone to pray, I would say just simply talk to God the way you would talk to your friends. Start small like thanking God for waking you up in the mornings. You can also ask Him how He is doing. Ask Him for protection. Take the small steps to change like letting someone over in traffic or opening the door for someone else, or maybe paying for someone's Starbucks. These are small steps anyone or at least those who are willing to change can make.

MOMENT OF REFLECTION:

Take a moment to reflect upon how you can change, if you even want to change, for the better. There are areas in life where improvement is needed. This can sometimes be a tough conversation that can be held because it requires looking within you. Yes, at times, it can be easier for others to tell you what the areas are that can be improved upon. But, when you look within yourself, then you can uncover the masks and rip off the scars of yesterday. If you are looking for a place to start, stare in the mirror. You stare into that mirror until the reflection starts looking back at you, and then the uncovering can begin. It may startle you but let it. It may also take some time to do this. It's ok.

CHAPTER 4

BE HUMBLE

This chapter is what I consider to be the core chapter. Being humble. For many years, I would hear my grandparents pronounce it as 'umble', omitting the 'h'. I asked questions as to why they pronounced it without the h and they only said that is the way they were taught to say it.

Here is what that is saying to me: My parents' generation only knew that humility means being submissive or being grateful for what you have. Now, my grandparents' generation were the ones that defined humble as 'don't make the white man mad', and, my great grandparents, who were a few years removed from slavery, still had that mentality of master-servant.

How does one become humble? Humbleness is often viewed as when someone lays down and just takes what people give to them. But that is not what humbleness is. Humbleness is also thought of as when a person does what people say without question. That is also not what humbleness is. Humbleness may also be thought of when a person doesn't have a thought about what they are being taught and they just accept what is. This too, is not what humbleness is. Humbleness is simply knowing that you can behave in a certain manner and not doing it. Humbleness is also when a person yields their will to the will of the other party, even though the person who needs to be humbled, may be of higher stature in relation.

Humbleness is also when someone subdues the way they think about themselves. In Romans 12:3 it states, "For I say, through the grace given to me, to everyone who is among you, not to think of himself more highly than he ought to think, but to think soberly, as God has dealt to each one a measure of faith."

Being humble will get a person far in life. Oftentimes, I think about how people become successful and it is by being humble. When I look at award shows such as the Grammy's or the Emmys, the recipient often says, "I am grateful and humble enough to receive this award."

Humbleness allows a person to become teachable. Humbleness allows a person to be coachable. Humbleness allows a person to become reachable. This is important because this is a HUGE step in becoming a success. Let us look at each of these 'able's'.

Humbleness allows a person to become teachable. When I think about being teachable, I think about someone who doesn't know how to do a certain task seeking out the knowledge to accomplish it. In seeking out knowledge, a person may either go on the internet, go to school, or seek out an individual who has the knowledge to help them. This is a tough thing to do especially if you are of a certain age, have lived life, and also taught others how to do this. It takes humility to accomplish this.

Another form of humbleness that I think of is those who are not Americans, who decided to master the language and are able to have jobs, and houses and graduate from colleges. I have patients who are like this. It takes a supreme form of humbleness because these individuals were of prominent status such as potentates in their country, doctors, and or nurses in their country. They have accomplished great successes in their lives only to come to America to start all over again. This is a huge challenge. Once again, it takes a huge amount of humility, something that I am striving for. Another 'able' that I will be discussing will be coachable. If a person is teachable, then they are coachable. Being coachable is nothing more than someone showing a person hands-on, guiding them to what they are asking them to do that will create the expected end. It is like playing a sport. That person has learned about what the sport is at first. Let's take football. If someone knows about football, I needed to know more about it because my son played football. He was on offense in the beginning. He played the center. His job was to hike the ball to the quarterback and to protect the quarterback. He had to be taught that position because he played on the defense as a safety and also as a lineman. He was so good that he helped his team to go to the finals. To achieve this, he had to be coachable. Coming from being teachable you are now coachable because teachable is giving you the information while coachable is applying the information.

The last 'able' is reachable. Being reachable means that an individual did not get the big head, meaning, they are not so full of pride that when asked something of someone, they will do it. Let me put it another way. They are not snobby about being asked to do something. They were humbled enough and gracious enough to do what they were being asked to do. Being reachable means that they can be touched by those who need their guidance and support. Being reachable means that an individual can be spoken to, can be seen, and are not all into the glitter and high and mighty mindset.

I have often been told to not toot my own horn. I would ask that individual why they would say such a thing to me and they simply said that no one wants to hear your accomplishments. So, what did I do? I just didn't tell that individual anything that I was doing. I simply continued to operate in the 'able's' which are teachable, coachable and reachable.

If I were to empower someone to become humble and operate in humility, I would simply say operate in the 'able's'. I say 'able's' because if an individual is willing, then they are able. This statement pretty much sums up what I said earlier. If an individual is teachable, then they are coachable.

MOMENT OF REFLECTION:

Being humble is a task that only those who want it will do. Being humble means that an individual is operating in the 'able's' which are teachable, coachable and reachable. Take a moment to reflect on when being humble paid off. Find ways to ensure being humble is a permanent part of your character.

CHAPTER 5

GIVE YOUR TITHES

Think about this: where can you live, visit, eat, study, or do anything for free besides your parents' house? Even that's a maybe because I paid rent at my parent's house at the age of 16.

Let's find out what exactly is a tithe. The first time I learned about the tithe was in church. The word tithe can be used as a noun that says that one-tenth of annual produce or earnings, was formerly taken as a tax for the support of the church and clergy. Another definition of a tithe being a noun also says a tenth of a specified thing. So, in other words, the actual tithe is a substance that can be a thing.

What is so significant about tithe? It shows honor, it shows respect and it shows understanding. How does a person show honor when giving tithe? I will answer by stating a correction. Oftentimes, people will say pay tithes. This seems like tithes are an actual bill and that the 'church' is the business that provides the bill. This is not the case. In showing honor, you are honoring

God. Now, God does not need your money, He needs your obedience. He desires your faith. He needs you to complete His mission on earth. His mission is to take care of the widows, orphans, and the least of these. What is meant by the least of these?

The least of these means that there are people who do not have what you have in terms of basic needs. Basic needs such as food, shelter, and clothing to say the least. In taking care of the widows, do we know that there are men and women widows, young and seasoned widows? What if the widow has young children, is the 'church' willing to step in and help with the children?

Will the widow need assistance at home like grass cutting or small handy jobs around the house? I know that they have the option to hire professionals to do those jobs which some widows and those who aren't widows do, including myself, but it shows care and concern from the 'church'. Going to see the sick and shut-in, or those who are in the hospital, also shows care and concern.

In taking care of the orphans, there aren't any orphanages, but there are shelters and there are foster homes. When a 'church' goes out and gives to foster homes, has toy giveaways, or adopts a school, the 'church' is still taking care of the orphans. Some even have scholarships for those children. And guess what...this all takes the tithe to accomplish this.

Another reason for the tithe is that when one goes to the 'church', or place of worship, it can be a synagogue, a mosque, or a hotel ballroom. When a person goes there, the lights are on, the temperature is comfortable, the sound system works, and the place of worship should be clean. It takes money to make all these things happen.

In showing respect, when giving the tithe, a person is respecting the work that is needed to be done in the house of worship. Just like most homes, it needs to be cleaned. Cleaning may require a mop bucket, a vacuum cleaner, and individuals to do what is needed to keep the place of worship clean.

These things take money, they take time and they take treasure. Why are these things mentioned here? They are mentioned here because of their importance. Why are time, talent and treasure important? What does being a parking lot attendant, mopping a floor, or operating a vacuum cleaner have to do with time, talent and treasure? I can answer that with a couple of scenarios.

If an individual attends a place of worship and doesn't have any money but wants to help out their community by helping the 'church', they can do so by giving their time. They can volunteer for the place of worship. Another person may not understand the concept of giving tithes, but they still want to help out. Time is one commodity that cannot be given back. A person can get back money, they can even get their talent back, but time is something that once it's gone, it is gone.

Let's talk about time. Time is something that will always move forward, it will never go backward. What do I mean? For example, with money, it can go backward, meaning operating in the red. This is a deficit. In business, this is not a good thing to operate in. However, given time, resources, and a plan, it can grow back, meaning, move forward. Time does not. Once it is spent, it will not come back. It is something that will keep moving forward. Time is also something that everyone gets, equally. Unless someone is no longer with us, everyone gets the same 60 seconds which is a minute, the same 60 minutes which is an hour, the same 24 hours which is a day, the same 7 days which is a week, the same 365 days which is a year. Now, how someone spends that time is totally up to them.

With time, it is so easy to splurge because we think that we have the time. This should not be the case because time is such a precious commodity. It is something that if not managed correctly, can easily be gone. In giving time to a worthy cause, that time can be so meaningful. It is here that time can be rewarding and encouraging. Time is something of the essence so when someone is giving their time to the community, that should be regarded as precious. There is respect when someone is giving their time and it should be revered because they are giving to the ministry the only thing that cannot be given back. It is something that is needed because when someone is giving of their time, it means that they care about you or your cause. It shows that the person who gave of their time is in agreement and is in submission to the cause. There is another caveat and that is time and talent can be viewed as one and the same.

There was a time in my life when I became homeless. It was myself and 2 of my 3 children when this ordeal happened. I grew up in the 'church' and I knew that God was my help. At this time, I was a giver in 2 of the 3 areas that I previously discussed. I mentioned that I was only a giver of 2, which were talent and treasure, because I had that in abundance which means, I wasn't worried about losing talent and treasure for I knew that I was going to get them back. It wasn't until later that I realized time was something that I couldn't get back.

Do you know the one thing that I have found out about time? Time can be redeemed. What do I mean? Think of redeeming a coupon. A person receives or is given a coupon for a certain item. They go to the person or entity that the coupon can be used or redeemed and they realize that they either saved money or got that item for free. With redeeming time, it is giving back time. It is like time still moves, time is still being spent, but it will appear that time has stopped for what that person is doing. It is like giving back the time that was once lost. Time is a source that is constant, but is still moving. That is what is needed to become successful. Use time wisely and efficiently.

If I can empower you, I will say that time is of the essence. Time is a great and expensive entity. I would say to always use it to your advantage. Think of time as a precious jewel, that you never will place with other jewels, but put in a special case that only you can see. How do you do this? By regarding time as something so precious, that it cannot be wasted. You would not waste something precious. It would be protected. It would be nurtured and it would be honored. Time is a great and awesome source.

MOMENT OF REFLECTION:

Remember a point in your life when you wished that you could go back and change certain events that occurred in your life. Once you have done that, look at how far you have come. You can use that thought or feeling and use it to accomplish anything that you want it to accomplish. Use time to create or nurture your talent. Use time to increase your treasure and most importantly, use time creatively and respectfully.

CHAPTER 6

STAY CONNECTED TO THE SOURCE

This chapter is about staying connected to something that either charges you, makes you happy, encourages you, develops you, and holds you accountable. Is staying connected to the source important? To answer that question, look at it like this. Your cell phone has a charging cord. When using the cell phone, the battery will run down. It gives the battery indicator light that is either a color indicator or, the cell phone may have a percentage indicator. Either way, it is an indication that the cell phone needs to be connected to the source so that the phone's power will be back at 100%.

How does this equate to this book? First off, let us look at the word church. Remember earlier in the book when I put church in quotations? For many years, I thought that the church meant the building where I go to praise the Lord by reading my Bible and singing praises to Him. However, this is not true. THE CHURCH IS A LIVING, MOVING AND BREATHING

ORGANISM. Now, I don't know of any building or structure that lives or moves, lives or breathes. I thought that the 'church' was the only place where God resides, the building. I thought that the building was where Jesus Christ was going to come and the rapture would occur. I understood what my Pastor at the time was saying. But what I have found out is that the church is not the building.

So, what is the 'church'? Let's go back to when Jesus was with His disciples. In the Bible, there are several references about the 'church'. Matthew 16:18 states, "And I say unto thee that thou art Peter and upon this rock I will build My church and the gates of hell shall not prevail against it." This is Jesus Christ, the Son of the Living God, who also gave Himself for the church as stated in Ephesians 5:25.

So, why would Jesus Christ say to Peter that the gates of hell will not prevail against the Church? Tell me something, how would the gates of hell prevail against a building? I am almost pretty sure that hell will have nothing to do with a building. Jesus Christ will not have given His life for a building. So, for many years when I thought that the church was a building, I was in error.

In going further into this and going to a ministry that teaches me correctly, I was made aware that I AM THE CHURCH. Say it with me: I AM THE CHURCH! When Jesus Christ comes back to His Church that will appear to Him without a spot or wrinkle it will not be buildings floating in the sky up towards what we view as the location of heaven (and I am speaking in terms of the rapture which means Jesus Christ is coming back).

The 'church' is a human being, not a building. In Matthew 18:17, "And if he shall neglect to hear them tell it to the church: but if he neglects to hear the church, let him be unto thee as a publican". What is this verse saying? It is saying that if anyone has a situation that they need to discuss with the church, they should discuss it with the church. Now, how can anyone discuss anything with an inanimate object? Earlier in the chapters of this book, I discussed the components of communication, that is a message, a messenger, a sender, and a receiver. Now, how can someone communicate with an inanimate object unless they are recording themselves?

So, once I learned about this, I now say ministry. What does a ministry have to do with being or staying connected? Well, I was active in my ministry. I was and still am, a greater and on the personal prayer ministry. I was going through a bout of depression because I had just become an empty nester and I didn't want to stay in the state, meaning Maryland. This is the place where my dad transitioned. I was told that my mom needed me here. From what I was told, my mom would end up homeless or worse so I agreed to come home and help her. That was not the case. This beautiful lady, meaning my mom, was living her 'bestest' life. This woman was out all times of night, going on trips out of the country, and simply having fun.

I became depressed because I thought my mom didn't need me. Growing up, my mom treated me harsher than my brothers. That is a story for another book. So, those thoughts came back to me, at the age that I am now. I also became depressed because I wasn't where I wanted to be at this stage of my life. I should have been further along in my life instead of living in an apartment when I should be living in a house that is almost paid off. There's a lot more stuff that I thought about that made me depressed. Once I start down that road or go inside that rabbit hole, I stay there for a while. Yes, I even contemplated suicide while I was active in the ministry.

I stopped going to the ministry. What the ministry did was call me when they realized that I wasn't coming as often or not at all. They reminded me of how my presence in the ministry was missed. I was just serving unaware of who was watching me. They reminded me that I needed to stay connected.

When people get discouraged, depressed, or angry, they tend to isolate themselves from everyone. This is a trick of the enemy. Let's look at it in military terms. When there is a war, there are war tactics that can be implemented to gain a victory. The enemy will choke the supply lines and communication lines. What I mean by choke is that they will either cut or scramble the lines so that the other side will not have what they need to win the war. Some of the supplies are food, water, fuel, medical supplies, and other soldiers, just to name a few. Communication is vital in war. It tells what is going on while fighting or giving supplies. Communication also gives information as to where the enemy is. There are a myriad of uses for communication, these are just a few. It is with this tactic that the enemy will cause isolation. It is of vital necessity that the unit stays connected with the mission unit or what is called the rear. This is also the location where once this is done, they return to the rear to rest, replenish, and regroup to complete and get ready for another mission.

The mission in life is up to the individual. However, every mission or situation in life will cause some isolation, but the key is to not get too deep into isolation. This is a trick of the enemy. My ministry reminded me that I needed to stay connected. What am I staying connected to? I am staying connected to the people who love me. I am staying connected to hearing from God through my Pastor, sometimes in terms of confirmation and warning. Staying connected to the people who have been through what I have been through can, and have, helped me to get to the other side of my situation. Yes, God does talk to me. Sometimes, I don't want Him to and I say, don't want to listen.

What is the source that I am staying connected to other than people? I am also staying connected to love. I am staying connected to going to the place where I can hear from God because in isolation, I could not hear from God, I could not hear from my children or anyone who truly loves me because I didn't want to. I wanted to be consumed by what I was thinking which disconnected me from the Source.

Just as how the cell phone needs to be charged after so much usage, so do we. As people, we need to be recharged. Here is why we need to be charged by what I call the 3 R's which are Rest, Replenish and Regroup. These 3 keys are vital to coming out of isolation or avoiding isolation.

Question: When you are recharging the cell phone, where do you put it? Some people have a portable charger that will allow them to keep talking or working from their cell phone without putting it down. The spot where they choose to place the cell phone is always intentional. They know exactly where they put it. They also know how long it will take for the cell phone to be fully charged. This is what rest does. Rest will allow anything to go back to being 100%.

Rest will also cause growth. Rest will allow greater strength when the body or item is needed. Here is what I mean by that. In regards to the body, when it has rested and is using renewed energy to complete what it is assigned to do, the mind will come in and remind you of tasks that you previously attempted to do. It will tell you, "Hey, remember when you tried that task the other day? Yeah, you may want to try completing that task this way." If you know of a baby that is an infant, the majority of the time, they are sleeping. They sleep because their body is now growing. For instance, some babies wore a size 0-2 months at birth but at 2 months, they need to wear a size 4 months or 6 months. It appears that they grew overnight and, in all truth, they kinda did. As for the cell phone, it works the same way only the battery lasts a little longer. Rest is vitally important in combating isolation.

While you are resting, you are also replenishing. What are you replenishing? You are replenishing your energy supply. You are replenishing your mental capacity, and you are also replenishing your dreams, goals, and aspirations. This is what keeps things going. Even the earth had to rest in order to replenish itself. When the world was on lockdown during covid and when I did go outside to either walk or sit out on my balcony, I realized that there was no haze in the sky, meaning there wasn't a lot of pollution. Also, the days lasted a little longer then, regardless of daylight savings time. The trees were greener. Meaning, the earth rested and was able to replenish itself. There is a theme here, that rest and replenishment go hand in hand.

The third R is regrouped. Let's look at it from a military view. Once the supply chain reaches the desired location, both the convoy and the receiving location can regroup. Maybe there was turmoil along the way towards the receiving location, meaning, the convoy that is dropping off the supplies needs to regroup to figure out how they can avoid turmoil. The receiving location may need to regroup in figuring out how to disperse the supplies in a manner that they will not run out in a short time. But how does this apply to you? Glad you asked.

You see, regrouping is the last step in the 3 R process in staying connected. It is the final part and it is so very important. Let's just say that you were under stress and you had to take a vacation or just go relax. First, you realized that you were stressed so you decided to rest. That rest looks different to many people, however, you are taking a break from that stress. While resting, you are replenishing your mind, thought processes, and strength. Once that has been completed, you decide to go back into work or that stressful environment, change your approach, or have a different mindset about how you handle things. This is great because staying connected requires these things. Please understand that life, people, and circumstances will cause stress. Period. But it is how you and I deal with this stress. Also, staying connected is vital to your success and your life. By using the 3 R's, you and I will both be able to stay connected.

If I can empower you to stay connected to the source, there are a couple of steps that I want you to take:

1. Realize and acknowledge what the situation has presented to you. By doing this, you are giving yourself automatic accountability and authority over the situation.

It is like calling a spade a spade, you are calling it what it is.

2. Do the 3 R's which are Rest, Replenish and Regroup.
3. Stay connected. Stay at the place where you are happiest, where you can be yourself, where there is no stress, and where you can hear from God. If you are reading this book and you don't believe in God or you are not a Christian, then go to the place where you get great advice from and stay there.

Overall, stay connected to your source. My source is God. Everyone's sources are different. My take on it is this: as long as you are producing a good outcome, a positive outlook on life, and can live free from that stress or situation, or are better able to handle said situation, then that is your source. Stay connected to it.

MOMENT OF REFLECTION: (THIS MOMENT OF REFLECTION WILL BE DIFFERENT. I WILL ASK YOU QUESTIONS ABOUT A SITUATION THAT YOU WERE IN. IF YOU NEED HELP IN FINDING YOUR SOURCE, THEN YOU NEED TO PURCHASE THE WORKBOOK)

Take a moment and reflect on the time that you were in a particular situation. How did that situation make you feel? Once that situation made you feel a certain way, what did you do? How did you handle it? Before today, did you do any of these suggestions, and if you did, kudos to you. Don't stop. I would solicit you to write the answers to these questions down if you don't have the workbook, and answer them. Great Luck.

CHAPTER 7

FIND THE CHURCH WHO PRODUCES MILLIONAIRES

Ok, here we are at the end which is nothing more than a new beginning. Remember that the definition of a millionaire is someone who has an asset of a million dollars. Now, those millions may come by an inheritance, or by hard work. Either way, that individual is a millionaire. Now, I also stated that you are the church. What type of church you are is TOTALLY UP TO YOU! Remember that the church is not a building, but you can use the building to produce millionaires. How? Glad you asked.

I will answer this question by using music and myself as an example. I love R&B, which is the short term for rhythm and blues. I don't care if it is from the 1970's (which was the best R&B era), 1980's, or the 2000's, I will play it. I am also from DC, which means I love some Go-Go which is the music of DC. Now, if I were to go to the Kennedy Centre for an opera, there is a certain manner and a certain group of people that will attend the opera at the Kennedy Centre. I am not saying that I will not go, but I know that opera is not my cup of tea per se, but I will attend the Phantom of the Opera or Chicago. I will do that because I want exposure to other forms of music and different cultures. This is a good thing. At the Kennedy Centre, I can't be charismatic, or act in an overly charismatic way at that particular event because it is not called for. I am naturally a charismatic, outgoing, overly encouraging person, in other words, loud. But I'm happy loud.

On the other hand, if I were to go to a club that plays R&B or to my family's house, I will more than likely be me. I can be overly charismatic and loud because they accept me as I am. I am understood by my family. Well, it is the same with a ministry. Find your place where you can be yourself. Find a place where you can be free to be understood. Find you a ministry where you are not ashamed, ridiculed or belittled. Unfortunately, some families operate in this manner, and for that I say continue to be yourself.

When finding a ministry, it should feel like you are part of a family. This is important because there is someone who is the head of the ministry and that person is either a Pastor, Priest, or Father. Sometimes, they provide a set of instructions. The question is, are you willing to follow them? Just remember that they are human beings that are prone to mistakes.

Here is where being humble comes into play. With family, there are times when we have to allow our family members to just be them. If they are difficult, I understand that that is them, not me. If they are full of hatred, it is them, not me. If they are loveable, it is them and me. It should be a goal to connect with people who have your answer, not your problem. This is the key aspect in finding the place that will allow the production of millionaires.

When looking for or finding your place, what are the qualities or aspects that you are looking for? Do you have a checklist? Are you looking for a place that is drama-free and not abusive? That is ok, but a person needs to make sure that the place that they attend is something that they want to come back to. A place that is full of love. A place where you don't want to leave, but want to kick your shoes off and simply relax. A place where you will have those Ah-ha moments.

Now, I am going to talk about the places or ministries that aren't warm and accepting. If you go into a ministry and the Pastor is looking better than everyone else, dressed in name-brand everything and blinged out in jewelry on every finger while the family and the parishioners are struggling, wearing tattered clothes and driving busted cars, then that is not the place to be. Let me say it again...IF THE PASTOR IS DOING BETTER, AND I MEAN WAAAYYY BETTER THAN THE PEOPLE, THAT IS NOT THE PLACE TO BE! Please remember this: a ministry is not measured by the amount of stuff that it acquires but by the changed lives of its people.

Is it ok for a ministry to have stuff? Absolutely. I am not against a ministry or anyone having stuff but the resources should be used for helping people as stated earlier. Having stuff should be used to help those who are lost and those who need direction and motivation. Having stuff should be used as a motivational tool for those who don't have stuff so that they can know that it is attainable. It should be taught that having stuff in ministry, means serving those who need to be served.

How do you know if the ministry has changed lives? By the power of the testimony. There are times when people don't want to hear the testimonies of other people and that may be because the person who is sharing their testimony may be long-winded or they may be an elder, like a grandmother or grandfather. Testimonies are very important because there is nothing new with us, only new people. It is a miracle that people have survived many things, strange things, even things that have been so diabolical that listening to their testimonies will be a great learning tool. This is what having a testimony is supposed to do.

There was a time in my life that I was experiencing 'church hurt'. I was serving in the ministry. At this time, I was only doing the video ministry and working in the cafe shop. As I stated earlier, I have a naturally highly charismatic attitude. I am full of joy because I have already been through a lot. I was going through a divorce while experiencing homelessness. I was in the cafe shop and I was making people laugh. One of the parishioners yelled at me saying, "Why you childish?". Now, I have been out of the Army for like almost a year so I still had that stamina. This woman is 6'2. I just stood there because if I were to do something, I would be the one going to jail. I simply left the area and the ministry.

I was hurt and embarrassed but allow me to pour a little wisdom from what I learned from this. Embarrassment is a choice and hurt people hurt people. That was only one person, not the whole 'church'. I heard of this saying that hurt people hurt people, however, I didn't apply it until I started writing this book. I now understand that hurt people need to go to the hospital, meaning the ministry. The funny thing is she was where she needed to be, I was just the target of her misery. I am not saying that people need to hurt people, just understand that that is one person. That ministry changed my life. It allowed me to heal my broken heart and my children enjoyed going there. My children volunteered there and also got baptized and saved there.

This is what I meant by having a ministry changing the lives of people. Yes, they had land beyond land. They also had a school and buses. They used that stuff to serve food to the poor and created a safe place for children. They even helped people save their homes due to the economic collapse and had a college scholarship for those who were in need. These are examples of what a good ministry does. They are supposed to produce the millionaires that are needed on the earth. This is what is meant when they say that God uses people to complete His mission within the earth.

If I could empower you, I would simply say look for a group of people that you need. Do they share the same beliefs as you? Yes, there are horrible people everywhere so what better place for them to be at? That's right, in the ministry. Please remember, that the success of a ministry is not the amount of stuff that it acquires, but the changed lives that occur. I can go into further depth, but you need to purchase the workbook to gain a better understanding.

MOMENT OF REFLECTION:

If you need help in looking for a ministry, just think about a family atmosphere. What spiritual needs in your life and that of your family, are in need of? What type of services does the ministry offer to assist you in this life?

CLOSING REFLECTIONS

The main reason I wrote this book was to empower people who are looking for success while still giving God the glory. I also wanted to help others. It is also for those who don't have a higher belief. God wants you to be successful.

This book is important to me because I was confused about being successful. I love God and I still wanted to serve God. I was confused about what the church is and I wanted others to realize that the church is them. I hope that my readers will understand that they are the church that can become successful.

This book has transformed my life in ways that I never in my wildest dreams could accomplish. It helped me to understand why God needs people to make sure His mission will be accomplished on earth. It has transformed my way of thinking in that we are the answer in the earth.

If I were to do a call to action, it would be to analyze where you are in your life right now. Where do you see yourself? Have you allowed God to be a source of your success, or are you doing it alone? Remember that with God, time will be redeemed.

My final message to you, the reader, will be to use this book as a tool. Do the work with the accompanying workbook to really open up and create a pathway towards success. It is my deepest and sincerest thoughts that are in this book. I hope that this book will transform your life the way it transformed mine.

DISCUSSION QUESTIONS:

What is a millionaire as defined in this book?

What is salt and how is it used?

What is faith and how can you use it?

Define prayer and how can it be used?

What is meant by being humble?

Do you pay tithes or give tithes? What is the difference?

Why do you need to be connected to the source?

Hurt people hurt people. Please explain this.

ABOUT THE AUTHOR

Dr. Sandra N. King is a native Washingtonian and a mother of 3 beautiful children. Ms. King is the author of "Singality, the Art of Being Single." She is a United States Army Veteran and has an organization called The Jesse King Foundation for Education where she believes that children can become what they want to become with the assistance and guidance of adults.

Her main focus is to help people who have been hurt and who are in pain to use that to their advantage to make a difference and place them in a different, better place. Places where they have never even thought about being before.

Dr. King is a person who motivates people. She strongly believes that everyone has a story and that their story can help others. She has her Doctorate in Theology and is a licensed minister.

Dr. Sandra can be reached at **www.drsandranking.com**.

NOTES: